Double Bass Exam Pack

ABRSM Initial Grade

Selected from the 2020–2023 syllabus

Name

CW00501399

Date of e.

Contents

Double Bass consultant: Cathy Elliott
Footnotes: Anthony Burton and Kathy Blackwell

Other pieces for Initial Grade   PF/DB *with piano or double bass accompaniment*

LIST A
4   **Catherine Elliott** Rondo Duo (*upper part; ending at b. 24*). *The Essential String Method, Double Bass Book 2* (Boosey & Hawkes) PF/DB
5   **Trad.** Twinkle Duet, arr. Elliott (*upper part*). *The Essential String Method, Double Bass Book 2* (Boosey & Hawkes) PF/DB
6   **Peter Furniss** Round and Round (*starting at letter B*). No. 8 (not 8a) from *In Concert: Brilliant Solos for Beginner Bass* (Da Capo)
7   **Katrina Gordon** Twittering Sparrows: No. 7 from *Feathered Friends* (Recital Music)
8   **Trad.** Down by the station, arr. Elliott. *Ready Steady Go* (Bartholomew)
9   **Trad.** The Jolly Miller, arr. Elliott. *Ready Steady Go* (Bartholomew)
10 **Trad.** Miss Mary Mac, arr. Lillywhite, Marshall, Hussey & Sebba. *Abracadabra Double Bass, Book 1* (Collins Music) PF/DB

LIST B
4   **Catherine Elliott** Swan Song. *The Essential String Method, Double Bass Book 2* (Boosey & Hawkes)
5   **Peter Furniss** So Slow. No. 7 (not 7a) from *In Concert: Brilliant Solos for Beginner Bass* (Da Capo)
6   **Katrina Gordon** Flight of the Swallows: No. 5 from *Feathered Friends* (Recital Music)
7   **Thomas Gregory** Footprints in the Snow. *Vamoosh Double Bass, Book 1* (Vamoosh)
8   **Sheila Nelson** Lullaby: No. 12 from *Right From the Start for Double Bass*, arr. Elliott (*slurs optional*) (Boosey & Hawkes)
9   **Sheila Nelson** Swingalong (*'E' version*). P. 18 from *Tetratunes for Double Bass* (Boosey & Hawkes) PF/DB
10 **Trad. French** Au clair de la lune, arr. Lillywhite, Marshall, Hussey & Sebba. *Abracadabra Double Bass, Book 1* (Collins Music) PF/DB

LIST C
4   **Jan Faulkner** Bowling Along: No. 1 from *First Bass* (*slurs optional*) (Recital Music)
5   **Jan Faulkner** Raggy Times: No. 4 from *First Bass* (Recital Music)
6   **Thomas Gregory** Walk on Mars! (*slides optional; observing DC, as in accomp.*). *Vamoosh Double Bass, Book 1* (Vamoosh)
7   **Sheila Nelson** Don't Bother Me: No. 13 from *Right From the Start for Double Bass* (Boosey & Hawkes)
8   **Sheila Nelson** Manchester United (*'E' version; with 1st repeat*). P. 28 from *Tetratunes for Double Bass* (Boosey & Hawkes) PF/DB
9   **Sheila Nelson** Off We Go!. *The Essential String Method, Double Bass Book 1* (Boosey & Hawkes) PF/DB
10 **Tony Osborne** Russian Circus. *The Really Easy Bass Book* (Faber)

First published in 2019 by ABRSM (Publishing) Ltd,
a wholly owned subsidiary of ABRSM, 4 London Wall Place,
London EC2Y 5AU, United Kingdom
© 2019 by The Associated Board of the Royal Schools of Music
Distributed worldwide by Oxford University Press

Unauthorised photocopying is illegal
All rights reserved. No part of this publication
may be reproduced, recorded or transmitted
in any form or by any means without the
prior permission of the copyright owner.

Music origination by Julia Bovee
Cover by Kate Benjamin & Andy Potts, with thanks to Brighton College
Printed in England by Halstan & Co. Ltd, Amersham, Bucks.,
on materials from sustainable sources.

Canada - Sleigh Ride

from *More Travel Tunes*

Margery Dawe

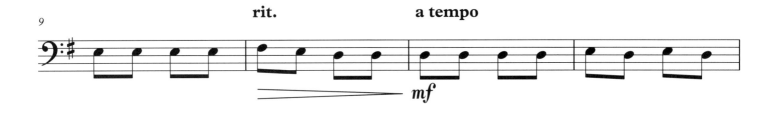

Think about a cold snowy scene as you play this bright and happy piece by Margery Dawe. The short notes and the lively tempo suggest that the sleigh is speeding quickly downhill.

© 1965 J. B. Cramer & Co. Ltd
This adaptation © 2019 J. B. Cramer & Co. Ltd
Adapted for Double Bass by Cathy Elliott by permission of Cramer Music Ltd.

Fish Cakes and Apple Pie

Sheila M. Nelson
(born 1936)

This lively piece comes from *Tetratunes*, a book by the composer and string teacher Sheila M. Nelson. All the pieces in this book use four notes that move up or down by step. The title 'Fish Cakes and Apple Pie' can be sung to the rhythm of the opening bars and this rhythm gives the piece its energetic feeling. All dynamics are editorial suggestions only.

A:3

New Toy

No. 9 from *Microjazz for Starters*

Christopher Norton
(born 1953)

The composer Christopher Norton was born in New Zealand and has written many pieces in pop, rock, and jazz styles for many different instruments. The bright and jaunty rhythm of this piece suggests the excitement of having a new toy to play with. Although the composer's metronome mark is ♩ = 170, students may prefer a slower tempo, for example ♩ = c.138.

© Copyright 1992 by Boosey & Hawkes Music Publishers Ltd
This adaptation © Copyright 2019 by Boosey & Hawkes Music Publishers Ltd
Adapted for Double Bass by Cathy Elliott by permission of the publishers.

Silent Friends

B:1

Thomas Gregory
(born 1973)

Thomas Gregory is a cellist, conductor and teacher from London. He says that the title *Silent Friends* 'refers to the treasured friendships some share with their pets, toys or even imaginary friends'. This piece, specially written for ABRSM, can be played with other string instruments, as it appears also in the violin, viola and cello syllabuses.

B:2

Gone for Good

No. 12 from *Ten O'Clock Rock*

Edward Huws Jones
(born 1948)

The smoothly flowing phrases and the gentle piano part in this piece by Edward Huws Jones suggest a quiet and thoughtful scene. The tempo marking, 'Plaintively', means 'expressing sorrow or sadness' so think about the feeling you might have when something is lost.

All night, all day

 B:3

Arranged by Nikki Iles

Trad. Spiritual

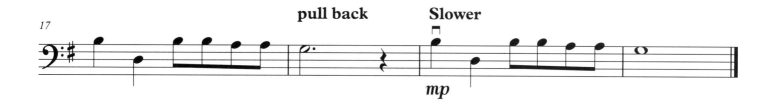

This piece is a spiritual, a type of religious song originally sung in the southern United States. The words of the chorus, 'All night, all day, angels watching over me, my Lord', can be sung to the music in bars 3 to 6.

C:1

Ten O'Clock Rock

No. 9 from *Ten O'Clock Rock*

Edward Huws Jones
(born 1948)

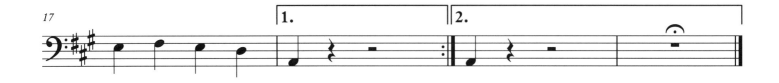

This lively piece by the British composer and teacher Edward Huws Jones is written with 'rock 'n' roll' style rhythms in the piano part. This gives the music its energetic character and drives it forward.

Double Bass Exam Pack

ABRSM Initial Grade

Selected from the 2020–2023 syllabus

Piano accompaniment

Contents

LIST A

1	**Margery Dawe** Canada – Sleigh Ride: from *More Travel Tunes*	2
2	**Sheila M. Nelson** Fish Cakes and Apple Pie	3
3	**Christopher Norton** New Toy: No. 9 from *Microjazz for Starters*	4

LIST B

1	**Thomas Gregory** Silent Friends	5
2	**Edward Huws Jones** Gone for Good: No. 12 from *Ten O'Clock Rock*	6
3	**Trad. Spiritual** All night, all day, arr. Iles	8

LIST C

1	**Edward Huws Jones** Ten O'Clock Rock: No. 9 from *Ten O'Clock Rock*	10
2	**Peter Martin** Hop Scotch: No. 2 from *Child's Play*	12
3	**Peter Wilson** Bow Rock: No. 4 from *Stringpops 1*	14

Double Bass consultant: Cathy Elliott
Footnotes: Anthony Burton and Kathy Blackwell

Editorial guidance

We have taken the pieces in this book from a variety of sources. Where appropriate, we have edited the pieces to help you prepare for your performance. We have added metronome markings (in square brackets) and the fingering and bowing indications have been amended where necessary to ensure a consistent approach within the album. Details of other changes or suggestions are given in the footnotes. Fingering, bowing and editorial additions are for guidance only: you do not have to follow them in the exam.

First published in 2019 by ABRSM (Publishing) Ltd,
a wholly owned subsidiary of ABRSM, 4 London Wall Place,
London EC2Y 5AU, United Kingdom
© 2019 by The Associated Board of the Royal Schools of Music
Distributed worldwide by Oxford University Press

Unauthorised photocopying is illegal
All rights reserved. No part of this publication
may be reproduced, recorded or transmitted
in any form or by any means without the
prior permission of the copyright owner.

Music origination by Julia Bovee
Cover by Kate Benjamin & Andy Potts, with thanks to Brighton College
Printed in England by Halstan & Co. Ltd, Amersham, Bucks.,
on materials from sustainable sources.

Canada – Sleigh Ride

from *More Travel Tunes*

Margery Dawe

Think about a cold snowy scene as you play this bright and happy piece by Margery Dawe. The short notes and the lively tempo suggest that the sleigh is speeding quickly downhill.

Fish Cakes and Apple Pie

Sheila M. Nelson
(born 1936)

This lively piece comes from *Tetratunes*, a book by the composer and string teacher Sheila M. Nelson. All the pieces in this book use four notes that move up or down by step. The title 'Fish Cakes and Apple Pie' can be sung to the rhythm of the opening bars and this rhythm gives the piece its energetic feeling. All dynamics are editorial suggestions only.

New Toy

No. 9 from *Microjazz for Starters*

A:3

Christopher Norton
(born 1953)

The composer Christopher Norton was born in New Zealand and has written many pieces in pop, rock, and jazz styles for many different instruments. The bright and jaunty rhythm of this piece suggests the excitement of having a new toy to play with. Although the composer's metronome mark is ♩ = 170, students may prefer a slower tempo, for example ♩ = c.138.

Silent Friends

Thomas Gregory
(born 1973)

Thomas Gregory is a cellist, conductor and teacher from London. He says that the title *Silent Friends* 'refers to the treasured friendships some share with their pets, toys or even imaginary friends'. This piece, specially written for ABRSM, can be played with other string instruments, as it appears also in the violin, viola and cello syllabuses.

B:2

Gone for Good

No. 12 from *Ten O'Clock Rock*

Edward Huws Jones
(born 1948)

The smoothly flowing phrases and the gentle piano part in this piece by Edward Huws Jones suggest a quiet and thoughtful scene. The tempo marking, 'Plaintively', means 'expressing sorrow or sadness' so think about the feeling you might have when something is lost.

© Copyright 1995 by Boosey & Hawkes Music Publishers Ltd
This adaptation © Copyright 2019 by Boosey & Hawkes Music Publishers Ltd
Adapted for Double Bass by Cathy Elliott by permission of the publishers.

All night, all day

B:3

Arranged by Nikki Iles

Trad. Spiritual

This piece is a spiritual, a type of religious song originally sung in the southern United States. The words of the chorus, 'All night, all day, angels watching over me, my Lord', can be sung to the music in bars 3 to 6.

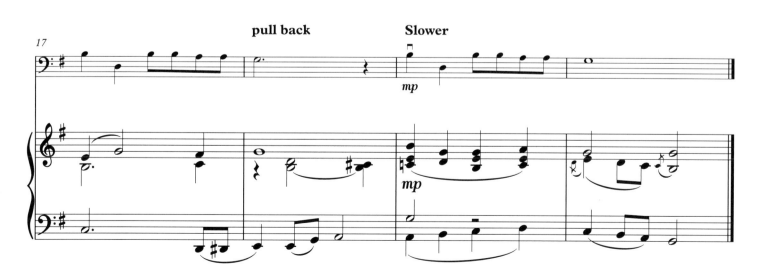

C:1

Ten O'Clock Rock

No. 9 from *Ten O'Clock Rock*

Edward Huws Jones
(born 1948)

This lively piece by the British composer and teacher Edward Huws Jones is written with 'rock 'n' roll' style rhythms in the piano part. This gives the music its energetic character and drives it forward.

Hop Scotch

No. 2 from *Child's Play*

Peter Martin
(born 1956)

With a swagger ♩ = 120

Hopscotch is a children's playground game in which players jump or hop between squares marked on the ground with chalk. The short accented notes and the quick string crossing in this lively piece by Peter Martin suggest the energetic hopping and jumping movements of the game. Although the composer's metronome mark is ♩ = 120, students may prefer a slower tempo, for example ♩ = *c*.108.

Bow Rock

No. 4 from *Stringpops 1*

Peter Wilson

This lively rock 'n' roll style piece was written by Peter Wilson. The music in bars 16–18 is like a loud conversation between the double bass and the piano. Although the composer's metronome mark is ♩ = 132, students may prefer a slower tempo, for example ♩ = *c*.120.

© 1987 by Faber Music Ltd, London WC1B 3DA
This adaptation © 2019 by Faber Music Ltd
Adapted for Double Bass by Cathy Elliott by permission of the publishers. All rights reserved.

Hop Scotch

No. 2 from *Child's Play*

Peter Martin
(born 1956)

Hopscotch is a children's playground game in which players jump or hop between squares marked on the ground with chalk. The short accented notes and the quick string crossing in this lively piece by Peter Martin suggest the energetic hopping and jumping movements of the game. Although the composer's metronome mark is ♩ = 120, students may prefer a slower tempo, for example ♩ = c.108.

AB 3950

C:3

Bow Rock

No. 4 from *Stringpops 1*

Peter Wilson

Go for it! ♩ = 132

This lively rock 'n' roll style piece was written by Peter Wilson. The music in bars 16–18 is like a loud conversation between the double bass and the piano. Although the composer's metronome mark is ♩ = 132, students may prefer a slower tempo, for example ♩ = c.120.

Scales

MAJOR SCALES

from memory
separate bows
even notes *or* long tonic, at candidate's choice

EVEN NOTES

to a sixth   ♪ = 76

D major

A major

LONG TONIC

to a sixth   ♪ = 76

D major

A major

Scales

MINOR SCALE

from memory
separate bows
even notes

to a fifth   ♪ = 76

E minor

Sight-reading

Sight-reading